# Can You Believe?

HURRICANES

by Sandra Markle
Illustrations by Jo-Ellen C. Bosson

SCHOLASTIC INC.

New York   Toronto   London   Auckland   Sydney
Mexico City   New Delhi   Hong Kong   Buenos Aires

For Myron, Genista, Jared, and Zachary Friesen

CAN YOU BELIEVE...

NOTE TO PARENTS AND TEACHERS: This book is intended to help children develop skills and concepts related to the following process (description drawn from the National Science Education Standards as identified by the National Academy of Sciences for K–4 students): "That weather changes form a pattern that can be used to analyze a hurricane's strength, predict the path it's likely to follow, and forecast where it is likely to cause damage." This is based on the following: "Weather changes from day to day and over the seasons. Weather can be described by measurable quantities, such as temperature, wind direction and speed, and precipitation."

Can you believe
these houses were destroyed by the sun?

These houses were blown apart by a **hurricane**, one of Earth's fiercest storms. When the sun's energy heats up one part of the ocean more than the area around it, a hurricane can begin to form. This book will let you investigate how that heat energy powers up a hurricane. You'll also learn why some hurricanes strike land and see the terrible damage some of these storms cause. Along the way, you'll discover lots of amazing facts about hurricanes—some may even seem unbelievable!

Like people, hurricanes have a life cycle.
They are born, grow stronger, weaken, and finally die.

So where in the oceans do you think hurricanes begin?

A. in the tropics
B. near the poles
C. at the equator

Turn the page and start exploring to find out!

Can you believe

hurricanes start in the tropics?

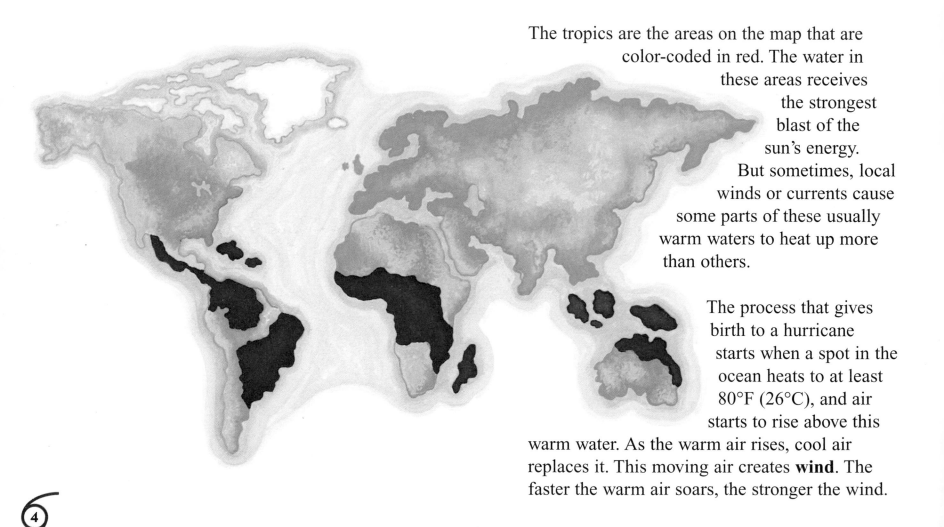

The tropics are the areas on the map that are color-coded in red. The water in these areas receives the strongest blast of the sun's energy. But sometimes, local winds or currents cause some parts of these usually warm waters to heat up more than others.

The process that gives birth to a hurricane starts when a spot in the ocean heats to at least 80°F (26°C), and air starts to rise above this warm water. As the warm air rises, cool air replaces it. This moving air creates **wind**. The faster the warm air soars, the stronger the wind.

TRY IT YOURSELF!

Watch how the process of warm air rising can start a hurricane.

1. Slip the mouth of a balloon over the neck of an empty soft drink bottle.

2. Set the bottle in a pan of hot tap water.

Ask your parents for help, so you don't burn yourself on the hot pan.

How Does It Work?

Air, like everything around you, is made up of tiny particles called **molecules**. When air is cold, the molecules move slowly and pack closely together. When air warms up, the molecules speed up, bump into one another, and spread apart. That makes the air take up more space than it did before, so the air rises out of the bottle. You can see this happening, because the rising air inflates the balloon.

This is the same process that takes place in the tropics. Like air, water is made up of molecules. As the rising hot air sweeps over the water, it warms some of the water molecules. These speed up and are knocked loose into the air. This process, called **evaporation**, adds **water vapor**, which is water in the form of a gas, to the air.

When the rising air is far away from the ocean's warmth, it cools down again. The water vapor cools, too. As the water molecules slow down, they collect on tiny particles of sea salt or dust. The vapor changes from a gas to tiny water droplets. This process, called **condensation**, creates **clouds**. It also releases heat energy. This energy warms the air again, making it soar upward even farther.

A thunderstorm forms when warm, moist air rapidly rises high enough to cool, forming clouds and rain. If there is enough warm, moist air rising, a cluster of thunderstorms may form. Then, if winds force the thunderstorms to move together, the storms merge into one storm system. When the winds in this system blow steadily at 75 miles (119 km) per hour, this storm is called a hurricane.

What shape do you think a hurricane takes?

A. funnel

B. pinwheel

C. bucket

Can you believe

a hurricane spins like a pinwheel?

Look at this **satellite** image of Hurricane Floyd. You can see the pinwheel cloud pattern created by spiraling winds. The clear center is the **eye**, where warm, dry air is surging downward. This moving air pushes out on the thunderstorms, shoving the closest ones tightly together. This forms a thick wall of clouds—the **eye wall**—where warm, moist air is soaring upward. The eye wall is where the storm's energy and its winds are strongest.

EYE WALL

EYE

What makes hurricanes start to spin?

A. the sun

B. Earth

C. the stars

Can you believe

Earth's turning makes hurricanes start to spin?

You probably know that Earth turns around and around. The force of this spinning is called the **Coriolis effect**. It starts the hurricane winds turning. Then the spinning winds sweep along the storm's bands of clouds.

TRY IT YOURSELF!

1. Mark a dot in the center of a paper plate and an X on the plate's rim.

2. Have a partner slowly turn the plate to the right as you draw a line between the dot and the X.

If the plate was held still, the line you would draw would be straight. Likewise, if Earth didn't rotate, air in a hurricane would flow directly from the outer edge in toward the storm's center. Just as turning your plate makes your line curve, the spinning Earth makes air start to circle around the storm's center.

DID YOU KNOW?

Hurricanes never form at the **equator**, the imaginary line stretching around the middle of Earth. The Coriolis effect is too weak at the equator to make storm systems start to spin.

Can you believe

some hurricanes grow to be much bigger than others?

Look how much bigger Hurricane Floyd (1999) was than Hurricane Andrew (1992).

DID YOU KNOW?

The word "hurricane" is only used when these super storms are in the Atlantic or West Pacific oceans. In the East Pacific and Indian oceans, they're called "typhoons." Scientists call all of these storms "tropical cyclones."

HURRICANE FLOYD

HURRICANE ANDREW

These maps show that Hurricane Floyd and Hurricane Andrew struck the United States in about the same place. Since it was bigger, Floyd caused damage over a much larger area than Andrew. The size of a hurricane depends on the amount of heat energy making the air and the water heat up and evaporate. The more heat energy there is, the bigger the hurricane gets.

What makes a hurricane move toward land?

A. waves

B. strong winds

C. other clouds

Can you believe

strong winds can push a hurricane onto land?

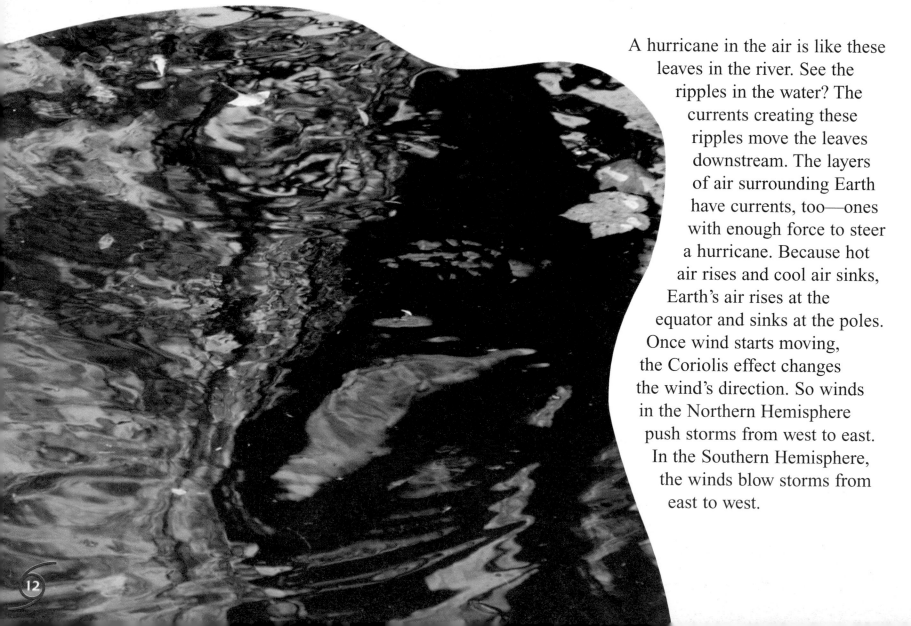

A hurricane in the air is like these leaves in the river. See the ripples in the water? The currents creating these ripples move the leaves downstream. The layers of air surrounding Earth have currents, too—ones with enough force to steer a hurricane. Because hot air rises and cool air sinks, Earth's air rises at the equator and sinks at the poles. Once wind starts moving, the Coriolis effect changes the wind's direction. So winds in the Northern Hemisphere push storms from west to east. In the Southern Hemisphere, the winds blow storms from east to west.

Hurricanes may travel long distances before they run into land. Satellites with cameras can show the size and shape of these storms. But forecasters must know how strong the hurricane will be when it strikes land. They also need to know when the hurricane will strike.

There is a hurricane season. It's summer through autumn, when seawater heats up most.

How do weather forecasters figure out where hurricanes are heading and what conditions are like inside the storm?

A. They use powerful telescopes.

B. They shoot laser beams into the storm.

C. They send people out to fly into the storm.

Can you believe
some people hunt hurricanes?

Hurricane Hunters from Keesler Air Force Base in Biloxi, Mississippi, fly into these fierce storms.

"You can't hear the wind over the plane's engine, but you can feel it. Passing through the bands of thunderstorms is as super bumpy as driving fast over speed bumps. It's very dark inside the hurricane, too, and raining so hard it sounds like tons of gravel is being thrown at the plane. Sometimes, there's so much water streaming down the windows it looks like we're in a submarine!"
—Major Valerie Hendry, weather officer for Hurricane Hunters

The Hurricane Hunters' plane is a flying lab, measuring the storm around it. There are sensors mounted on the outside of the plane. These sensors measure the weather conditions eight times a second.

The strongest winds are likely to be below the plane near Earth's surface. So, several times during a mission, the Hurricane Hunters drop a special tube with a parachute out of the plane. Packed with weather sensors, this tube reports on the air temperature, wind speed, and amount of water vapor in the air all the way to the surface of the ocean.

Georgia

Florida

CUBA

Here you can see Hurricane Floyd striking land in 1999. Weather forecasters use satellite photos and data from the Hurricane Hunters to make computer models. These models show where a hurricane is likely to travel, based on the paths followed by past hurricanes in the same area. If a hurricane is likely to strike land, people need to be warned.

Deciding when and where to issue a hurricane warning is a big decision. When a city gets a hurricane warning, windows that could break have to be boarded up. Anything that could blow around must be packed away.

People have to move out of the storm's path. Sometimes, people have to leave pets behind. These dogs were rescued from flooded buildings after a hurricane.

How strong are hurricane winds?

A. They can blow apart buildings.

B. They can drive a board through a tree trunk.

C. They can uproot trees.

Can you believe

hurricanes are strong enough to do all these things?

Some hurricanes are stronger than others. Scientists have created a scale to rate a hurricane's strength from 1 to 5—weak to strong.

Category	Wind Speed	Possible Damage
1	74–95 mph (119–152 kph)	Causes minor damage to trees, shrubs, and mobile homes
2	96–110 mph (154–176 kph)	Causes major damage to mobile homes; blows off roofs; blows down trees
3	111–130 mph (178–209 kph)	Destroys mobile homes, damages small buildings
4	131–155 mph (210–249 kph)	Heavy rains cause flooding; damage to homes and buildings
5	156+ mph (251+ kph)	Heavy damage to homes and buildings; heavy flooding

Look at the damage Hurricane Andrew did! This Category 4 hurricane peeled off roofs and tossed cars through the air. Loose boards zoomed through the air as fast as bullets. The wind even carried heavy steel beams from damaged buildings several blocks before crashing them into other buildings.

DID YOU KNOW?

In the United States, Florida is the state that has been struck most often by hurricanes.

The most deadly hurricane to ever hit the United States struck Galveston, Texas, in 1900, before there was an effective warning system. On Saturday, September 8, 1900, the Weather Bureau in Washington, D.C., sent Galveston a telegraph message warning that a dangerous hurricane was coming. Few heard about the warning. Many of those who heard didn't believe it. At the time, the weather was still fine. By late Saturday afternoon, though, the winds were raging. By then, it was already too late to escape.

Galveston is on an island two miles (3 km) from the coast of Texas. The storm's high seas had quickly flooded the bridges connecting the city to the mainland. By the time the hurricane swept inland, more than 2,000 homes—half the homes in the city—were destroyed. More than 6,000 people had been killed.

This chart shows where and when some of the deadliest hurricanes and typhoons struck during the twentieth century. After warning systems were improved, the largest loss of life was in poorer countries. Even an average hurricane does more damage there. It is harder for people to escape the storm, and buildings aren't usually built to withstand strong winds.

Location(s)	Year	Name of Hurricane	Number of Deaths
Honduras, Central America	1998	Mitch	10,000
Haiti, Florida, Dominican Republic, Costa Rica	1994	Gordon	1,145
Bangladesh	1991		100,000
Dominican Republic, United States	1979	David	2,068
Honduras, Nicaragua	1974	Fifi	8,000
Bangladesh	1970		300,000
Cuba, Haiti	1963	Flora	8,000
El Salvador, Honduras	1934		3,000
Cuba, Cayman Islands, Jamaica	1932		3,107
Dominican Republic	1930		8,000
Galveston, Texas	1900		6,000

Data on Atlantic storms by Jack Beven/NOAA; Data on Bangladesh typhoons by National Hurricane Center/NOAA

DID YOU KNOW?

During World War II, the U.S. Army Air Corps and Navy weather forecasters named hurricanes after their wives or girlfriends. Starting in 1979, hurricanes were also given male names. Each year, forecasters give the first storm a name starting with "A," and then go through the alphabet in order. But if your name starts with Q, U, X, Y, or Z, you will never have a hurricane named after you. There are so few names starting with these letters that they're never used.

A hurricane slammed these ships onto the beach. But it wasn't the strong winds that caused this damage. So what did?

A. waves

B. hail

C. tornadoes

Can you believe giant waves pushed these ships ashore?

Some of a hurricane's monster waves ride on a big dome of water called **a storm surge**, which can do a lot of damage. In 1969, Hurricane Camille, a Category 5 hurricane, smashed into Bay St. Louis on the Mississippi Sound with waves two and a half stories tall. No wonder that hurricane destroyed most of the houses along the beach!

TRY IT YOURSELF!

1. Fill a cake pan about half full of water.

2. Blow gently across the surface of the water.

Your breath pushing on the surface will pile up waves. Blow harder to make bigger waves. Imagine the big waves that strong hurricane winds create!

What happens when the giant waves created by a hurricane roll back into the sea?

A. Land washes away.
B. Waves get bigger.
C. Lightning strikes.

Can you believe

hurricane waves can wash away a beach?

If you've ever stood in the surf on a sandy beach, you know that when waves roll back into the sea, they carry away some of the sand. A hurricane's monster waves carry away *lots* of sand and soil. Sometimes, even trees that withstood the storm fall over, because after the storm there is not enough soil to anchor the tree roots. Land under buildings may be washed away, too. The building's walls may even crack. Then, buildings that survived the hurricane's winds break apart.

These before-and-after photos of Miami Beach, Florida, show how people protected coastal areas from a storm surge. Sand was pumped up from the sea bottom to make the beach much wider. This gives the waves more room to crash.

What other water worries can hurricanes cause?

A. snow
B. ice
C. dew

Can you believe

the holes in this house were punched by ice?

These holes were made by balls of ice called **hail**. The hail started to form when water droplets inside the hurricane clouds were carried very high into the air. There, the air was so cold the drops froze. As the little balls of ice fell through the clouds, the outer surface melted and it picked up another coating of water. Next, strong winds nearer the surface tossed the hail back up again, freezing its new water coat. This process was repeated several times, adding layer upon layer of ice. The stronger the winds, the bigger the hail became. Finally, the hail was too heavy for the winds to toss up, and the ice balls dropped like stones. Hail from hurricanes is rare, though, because the warm air usually melts the ice before it reaches the ground.

Hurricanes sometimes give birth to other very powerful storms—tornadoes. Like a spinning vacuum cleaner hose, a tornado sucks air in the bottom and shoots it upward. A tornado sucks up anything in its path—trees, roofs, cows, cars, and dirt. Worse still, the bands of thunderstorms in a hurricane may produce a group of tornadoes. Imagine the damage Hurricane Gilbert caused in 1988 when it spawned about 40 tornadoes in Texas!

A hurricane also carries water inland as rain. A hurricane dumps water so fast that the water doesn't have time to soak in. The rainwater streams off lawns, fills up streets, and pours down storm sewers.

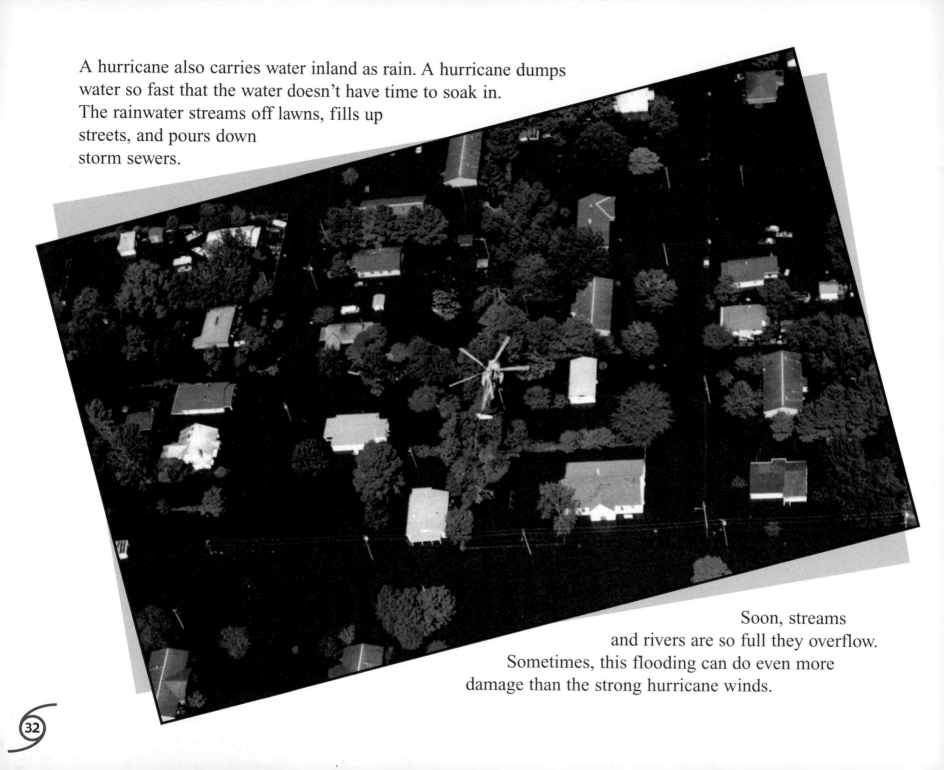

Soon, streams and rivers are so full they overflow. Sometimes, this flooding can do even more damage than the strong hurricane winds.

You may be surprised to learn that the evacuation plan for New Orleans is up, not out. So much of this city is below sea level that a hurricane's storm surge could cause terrible flooding. Roads might be underwater, too. Instead of encouraging people to leave New Orleans when a storm arrives, city planners have identified the strongest tall buildings so people can take shelter above flood level.

Amazingly, one part of a hurricane is calm and clear. Can you guess what it is?

A. eye

B. eye wall

C. storm surge

Can you believe

the air in the eye of a hurricane is calm and clear?

Usually, the hurricane's eye is about 20 miles (32 km) wide. Hurricane Hunter Major Valerie Hendry said, "Inside the eye, the sun's shining, and it's clear. All around the eye, though, you can see huge walls of clouds. It's like being inside a giant cloud stadium." The center of a hurricane is calm because the air rapidly descending in the eye pushes the storm clouds aside. Because the storm clouds are piled up around the eye, the eye wall contains the hurricane's strongest winds.

TRY IT YOURSELF!

You can see why the eye of a hurricane is so calm.

1. Fill a sink about half full of water and then release the plug.

2. Watch as the sink empties, and you'll see the water spiral around the drain.

Water rushing down the drain pulls air down in the center of the spiral. Like the hurricane's eye, the air pushes the water aside. So the eye of this water cyclone is clear, too. In fact, if you carefully put your finger straight down the center of this "water hurricane," it will stay dry.

What finally stops a hurricane?

A. sunlight
B. land
C. water

Can you believe

moving across land will stop a hurricane?

Rub your hand on a piece of carpet. The friction you feel is the same sort of drag that slows down winds blowing across land. After a hurricane blows over dry land, it also loses its heat engine—the heat given off when water vapor condenses. Without a fresh supply of water, rainfall slows down, too. Finally, the storm system breaks up into a cluster of thunderstorms and the hurricane is finished.

DID YOU KNOW?

In 1994, Typhoon John hung around for more than a month. Most hurricanes only last a few days.

How much power does a dying hurricane have?

A. no more than a gentle rainstorm

B. none

C. enough to wreak havoc for hundreds of miles

Can you believe

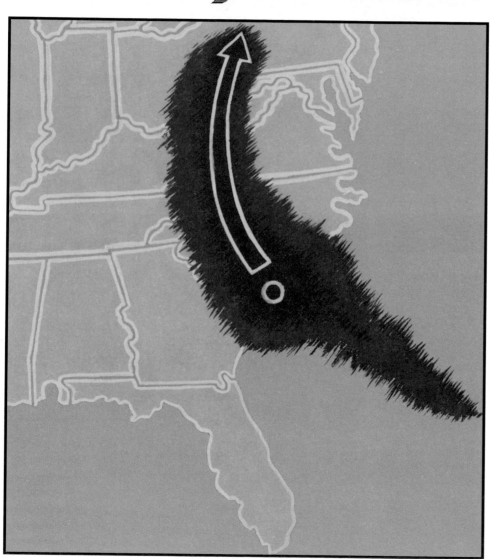

a dying hurricane can do damage far inland?

On September 21, 1989, Hurricane Hugo struck Charleston, South Carolina, wrecking buildings for a hundred miles (160 km) along the coast. Then it moved inland, downing trees and power lines and damaging buildings. Next, the storm plowed on, bringing heavy rains through central Ohio and western Pennsylvania. Before Hurricane Hugo was finished on September 25, it even damaged crops by causing early freezes as far away as Missouri and Arkansas.

After a hurricane ends, people have to work together to repair the damage. Often, people from nearby towns will help a community rebuild. Of course, it would be better if hurricane damage could be prevented entirely. Many people have come up with ideas about how to stop hurricanes.

Which of these ideas do you think people considered?

A. blow the hurricane out to sea
B. keep seas too cool to start a hurricane
C. blast the hurricane to bits

Can you believe

people thought all of these ideas would stop hurricanes?

You'll guess why these ideas were rejected.

Blow it away:

The plan was to build a line of windmills along the coast to blow approaching hurricanes back out to sea. Imagine what huge windmills would be needed to stop a strong hurricane!

Chilling the ocean:

The plan was to tow an iceberg into an area where a hurricane was forming. The berg would then cool the warm ocean water, stopping the process that gives birth to a hurricane. Think how hard it would be to tow a giant iceberg that far!

Dropping a bomb:

The plan was to drop a hydrogen bomb into a hurricane to blow the storm apart. But scientists realized the air currents steering the hurricane would quickly carry the bomb's deadly fallout over land.

Can you think of ideas that might really work to help people stay safe? Brainstorm!

Until scientists figure out how to stop hurricanes, people who live where hurricanes can strike have to be prepared. For example, the storm surge caused by hurricanes can be deadly. After the 1900 hurricane, survivors in Galveston, Texas, built a high wall along the edge of the ocean. When other hurricanes struck Galveston in 1915 and 1961, this seawall kept the city from being washed away. Other cities along the coast have built dunes, mounds of sand that act like a natural wall.

Metal straps are used to help keep buildings from blowing apart in hurricane-force winds.

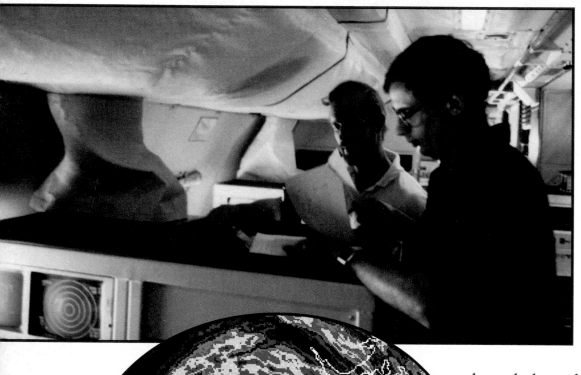

Here you can see Mark Powell and Frank Marks flying into a hurricane to check its strength. For years, Powell had studied the damage caused by hurricane winds. Then he discovered something. Strong winds produce foam on waves—the stronger the wind, the thicker the foam. Powell knew that radar, a tool that bounces radio waves off surfaces, was already being used to tell where rainfall was heaviest in a hurricane. So Powell took the radar on board a plane flying into a hurricane and aimed it down at the ocean's surface. Just as Powell had hoped, the radar showed where the ocean's foam layer was thickest. This lets him give weather forecasters new information to use in judging where the hurricane's strongest winds will strike land. This information also lets power companies, emergency crews, and insurance companies know where people will need the most help.

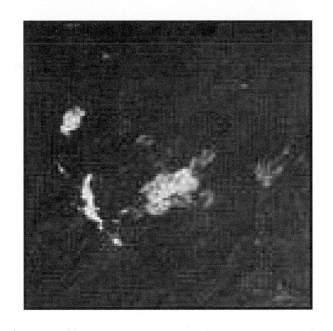

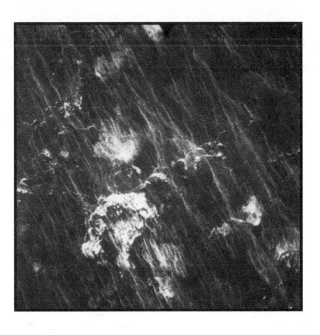

NORMAL WAVES   HURRICANE WAVES

Hurricane Challenge

Look at this image of normal sea waves. Then check out the waves created by a hurricane. What do you see that lets you know these waves were made by very strong winds?

Can you believe
hurricanes are part of Earth's natural processes?

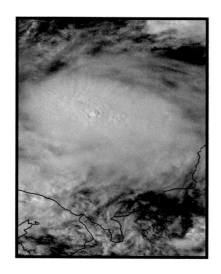

Thunderstorm clusters,
October 22

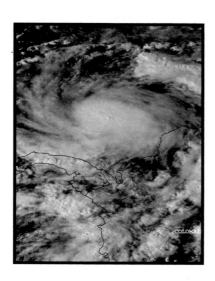

Early storm system,
October 25

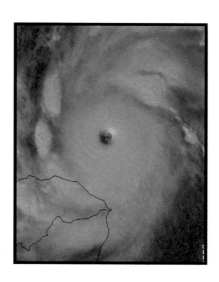

Strong cyclone,
October 26

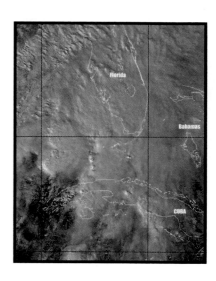

Thunderstorms,
November 4

Now that you know how the sun's energy and ocean water power up a hurricane, take a look at Hurricane Mitch's life cycle. The processes that caused all of these stages are really just part of what happens to mix warm and cool air all around Earth. You see this mixing every day in your own life. In a hurricane, though, this mixing creates destructive winds, monster waves, and damaging floods. So while hurricanes *are* part of Earth's natural processes, these super storms are what happens when those processes go wild!

Glossary/Index/Pronunciation Guide

cloud Visible mass of bits of water or ice in the air. 6, 8–9, 34

condensation [kahn den SAY shuhn] The process of water vapor losing heat and changing into liquid water. 6, 37

Coriolis effect [cohr ee OH less i fekt] The effect of Earth's turning on the motion of moving objects and hurricanes. 9

equator [ee KWAY tr] The imaginary line around the middle of Earth, midway between the North and South poles. 9, 12

evaporation [ee VAP er ay shun] The process of water changing from a liquid to a gas, water vapor. 6

eye Calm area in the center of a hurricane. 8, 34–35

eye wall The wall of clouds created by bands of thunderstorms surrounding a hurricane's eye. 8, 33–34

hail Balls of ice made up of overlapping layers of ice. 30

hurricane [HER uh kayn] Name given to a powerful storm system made up of spiraling bands of thunderstorms with wind speeds of more than 74 mph (119 kph). 2–46

molecule [MAHL uh kyool] Smallest particle of something that still has all of its features, such as a molecule of water. 5

satellite [SAT tuhl ite] An object scientists put into orbit around Earth to collect and send back information. 8, 13, 16

storm surge A high wave of water created by the uplifting pressure of the hurricane's eye. 26–27, 42

tornado [tor NAY doh] Very powerful windstorm with a spiraling, funnel-shaped cloud that usually only affects a small area but may cause a lot of damage. One or more may be spawned by the bands of thunderstorms in a hurricane. 31

water vapor Water when the molecules speed up, bump into each other, and form a gas. 6–7, 37

wind Air moving across Earth's surface. It forms when warm air rises and cool air rushes in to replace it. 4, 7–8, 14–15, 18, 21, 23–25, 32, 37, 43–45

PHOTO CREDITS
Cover: NOAA/NESDIS
p. 3: Shaw McCutcheon/Bruce Coleman
p. 7: Jim Edds
p. 8: NOAA/NESDIS
p. 10: NOAA/NESDIS
p. 11: NOAA/NESDIS
p. 12: Skip Jeffery
p. 13: NOAA/NESDIS
p. 14: Hurricane Hunters, 403rd Wing, Keesler Air Force Base, U.S. Air Force; Valerie Hendry
p. 15: Hurricane Hunters, 403rd Wing, Keesler Air Force Base, U.S. Air Force
p. 16: NOAA/NESDIS
p. 17 (2): FEMA
p. 18: Dave Martin/AP/World Wide Photos
p. 19: Impaled Palm, Roger Edwards; Damaged house, Jim Edds; Downed palms, Kike Calvo/Bruce Coleman
p. 21: Tony Arruza/Bruce Coleman/
p. 22: Rosenberg Library, Galveston, Texas
p. 23: Rosenberg Library, Galveston, Texas
p. 25: Timothy O'Keefe/Bruce Coleman
p. 26: Timothy O'Keefe/Bruce Coleman
p. 27: M.H. Black/Bruce Coleman
p. 28: FEMA
p. 29 (2): Joan Pope, U.S. Army Corps of Engineers
p. 30: House full of holes, Roger Edwards; Hail, Bruce Coleman/ Tony Arruza
p. 31: E.R. Degginger/Bruce Coleman
p. 32: FEMA
p. 33: FEMA
p. 34: AP/World Wide Photos/NOAA
p. 36: Bruce Coleman/Metzen
p. 37: Bruce Coleman/Metzen
p. 39: Jack Dykinga/Bruce Coleman
p. 42: Joan Pope, U.S. Army Corps of Engineers
p. 43 (2): FEMA
p. 44: Mark Powell; inset, NOAA/NESDIS
p. 45: Regular sea waves, Hurricane Hunters, 403rd Wing, Keesler Air Force Base, U.S. Air Force; Hurricane waves, NOAA/NESDIS
p. 46 (4): NOAA/NESDIS

Acknowledgments: The author would like to thank the following persons for sharing their expertise and enthusiasm: Roger Edwards, Meteorologist, Storm Prediction Center, Norman, Oklahoma; Dr. Mark Powell, Research Meteorologist, Hurricane Research Division, Atlantic Oceanographic and Meteorological Laboratory; Joan Pope, specialist in storm hydrodynamics and shore protection, U.S. Army Corps of Engineers, U.S. Army Engineer Research and Development Center; Dr. Norman W. Scheffner, Research Hydraulic Engineer with the Waterways Experiment Station, U.S. Army Corps of Engineers; Peter Dodge, Meteorologist, Hurricane Research Division, Atlantic Oceanographic and Meteorological Laboratory; and Major Valerie Hendry, weather officer, Hurricane Hunters, Keesler Air Force Base, Biloxi, Mississippi. As always, a special thanks to Skip Jeffery, for his help and support.

ISBN 0-439-35610-5

Text copyright © 2002 by Sandra Markle.
Illustrations copyright © 2002 by Scholastic Inc.

All rights reserved.
Published by Scholastic Inc., 555 Broadway, New York, NY 10012.
SCHOLASTIC and associated logos are trademarks and/or registered trademarks of Scholastic Inc.

12 11 10 9 8 7 6   4 5 6 7 8 9/0

Printed in the U.S.A.   40
First Scholastic printing, January 2002